ESPORT

ROCKET LEAGUE

KENNY ABDO

Fly!
An Imprint of Abdo Zoom
abdobooks.com

abdobooks.com

Published by Abdo Zoom, a division of ABDO, P.O. Box 398166, Minneapolis, Minnesota 55439. Copyright © 2023 by Abdo Consulting Group, Inc. International copyrights reserved in all countries. No part of this book may be reproduced in any form without written permission from the publisher. Fly!™ is a trademark and logo of Abdo Zoom.

Printed in the United States of America, North Mankato, Minnesota.
052022
092022

Photo Credits: Alamy, Getty Images, Shutterstock, ©The Bearded Clock p.cover / CC BY-ND 2.0, ©Bago Games p.4 / CC BY 2.0, ©VCU Capital News Service p.10 / CC BY 2.0, ©Official GDC p.16 / CC BY 2.0, ©Bago Games p.20 / CC BY 2.0
Production Contributors: Kenny Abdo, Jennie Forsberg, Grace Hansen
Design Contributors: Candice Keimig, Neil Klinepier

Library of Congress Control Number: 2021950293

Publisher's Cataloging-in-Publication Data

Names: Abdo, Kenny, author.
Title: Rocket League / by Kenny Abdo.
Description: Minneapolis, Minnesota : Abdo Zoom, 2023 | Series: Esports |
    Includes online resources and index.
Identifiers: ISBN 9781098228514 (lib. bdg.) | ISBN 9781644947876 (pbk.) |
    ISBN 9781098229351 (ebook) | ISBN 9781098229771 (Read-to-Me ebook)
Subjects: LCSH: Video games--Juvenile literature. | eSports (Contests)--Juvenile
    literature. | Automobiles, Rocket-powered--Juvenile literature. | Soccer--
    Juvenile literature.
Classification: DDC 794.8--dc23

TABLE OF CONTENTS

ROCKET LEAGUE

Mixing soccer with cars, *Rocket League* is a fast-paced esport that fans cannot get enough of.

Created by a small video game **developer**, Psyonix, the game and its players have become one of the most successful gaming communities in esport history!

BACKSTORY

Buy Now | Rocket Leag

🔒 Beveiligd | https:

PSYONIX

Psyonix had *Rocket League* in the works for more than two years.

e® – ○ ✕

www.rocketleague.com/buy-now-google/

OCKET
EAGUE.®

GAME INFO

The team at Psyonix wanted to combine sports with automobiles. That way the game could attract many different types of players and fans.

ROCKET LEAGUE

Rocket League **dropped** in 2015. It had more than 183,000 unique players within its first week!

JOURNEY

In March 2016, the first Rocket League **Championship** Series (RLCS) was announced. Team iBP closed out the finals winning the $27,500 prize!

The second **season** of the RLCS took place in December 2016. The team FlipSid3 Tactics walked away with the $125,000 prize pool!

For **Season** 3, Northern Gaming reigned supreme. RLCS Season 4 was the second **championship** series of 2017. Gale Force eSports edged out Method for the $50,000 prize!

Season 6 was held in 2018. It featured a million-dollar prize pool, which 1st place team Cloud 9 won $200,000 of. Paris-based team Renault Vitality was the victor of Season 7.

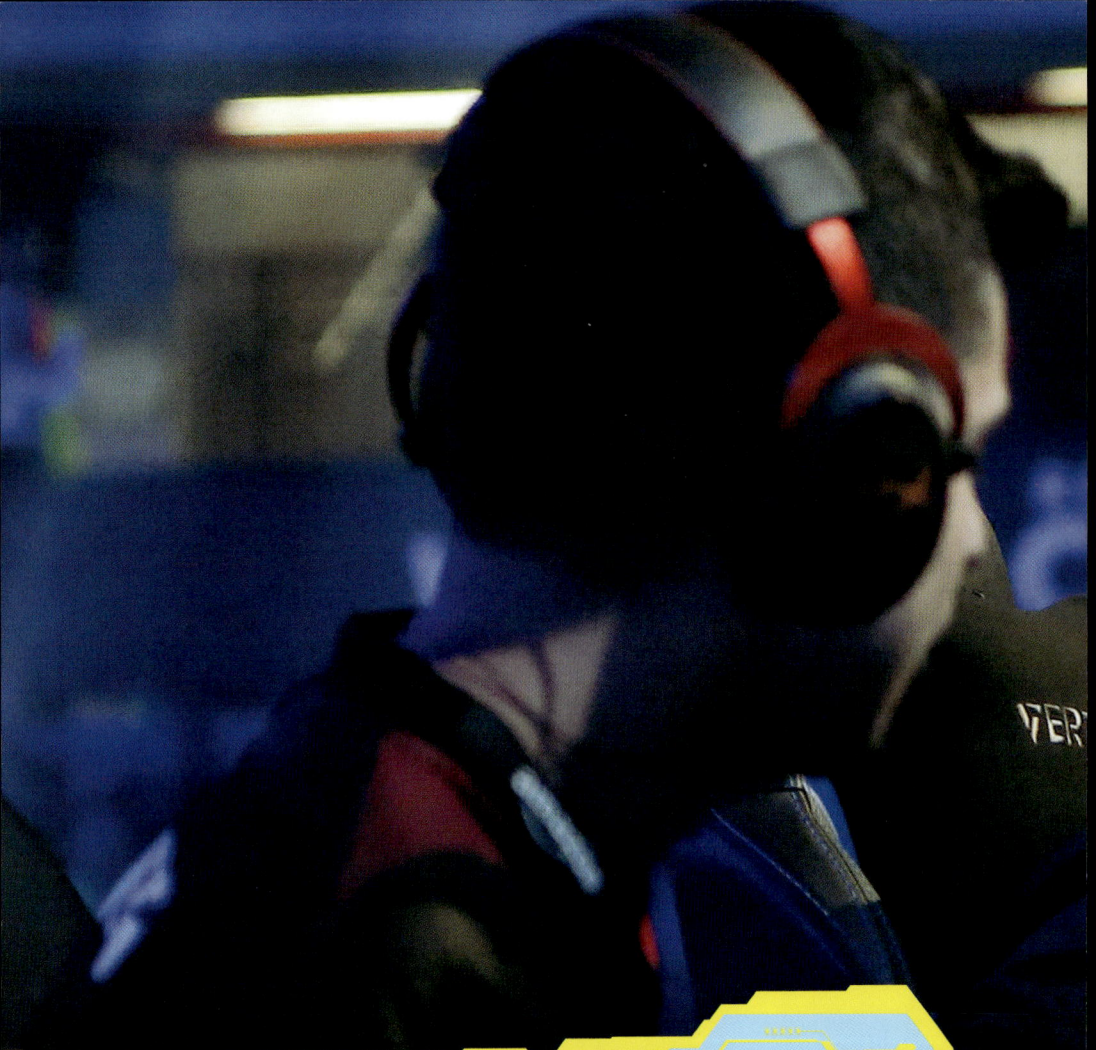

The **Season 9 championship** was cancelled due to the COVID-19 **pandemic**. Team BDS won RLCS X, defeating The General NRG. The team from Switzerland received a $90,000 first-place prize.

RLCS 2022 brought in the Middle East, North Africa, and Asia Pacific as new regions for play. There was a $6,000,000 prize pool, three international **Majors**, and a World **Championship** as well!

Rocket League has one of the most passionate esport fan bases around. By combining two things loved around the world, the game brings together fans and players alike, rocketing past all of the rest.

GLOSSARY

championship – a game held to find a first-place winner.

developer – a company that builds and creates software and video games.

drop – when something that is highly anticipated is released to the public.

Major – the biggest international tournament of the RLCS where 16 teams come together to face off for the title of Fall Major Champions.

pandemic – a widespread outbreak of disease that afflicts many people over different continents.

season – the portion of the year when certain games are played.

ONLINE RESOURCES

Booklinks
NONFICTION NETWORK
FREE! ONLINE NONFICTION RESOURCES

To learn more about Rocket League, please visit **abdobooklinks.com** or scan this QR code. These links are routinely monitored and updated to provide the most current information available.

INDEX